# Winning Back Your Treasures

## Ultimate Guide on how to Befriend Your Teens

Deborah Grace

# DEDICATION

This book is dedicated to all parents who desired to gain back their precious teenagers they have being disconnected from in one way or another.

# TABLE OF CONTENTS

# INTRODUCTION

Parenting and raising our teenage boys and girls comes with some struggles (for many of us) because their behaviors many times changes suddenly without us been ready and adequately prepared.

Many parents know their children age is increasing but their mind does not register that the increase means all around change in their children's life.

They usually treat their teenage like the under thirteen they use to be but become disappointed or troubled once they don't get the usual response. Our teenagers can suddenly become strangers to us in some ways we can't explain, they can readily swing mood like chameleon, changing color. Some become exceptional sensitive to words, people, places, etc. For most of them they begin to pay more attentions to their looks and their interest also changes.

All this experience leave parents exhausted and helpless because the precious baby we use to dote over has become someone we find a bit difficult to understand.

This book gives us practical and simple ways to win back our precious children.

# Book One

## Teenagers: what's up with them?

Teenage period is not very easy to deal with for parents or children.

Knowing what lies ahead made preparing for it easy. When parents have pre-knowledge of what teenager goes through dealing with teens become easy.

The only way to effectively help your teen at this stage is to understand what is happening within and about them and positively deal with it.

This greatly reduces insecure feelings and unstable emotions that is very common at this stage. Here are lists of common changes at this stage of life.

## 1. Body Changes

Because of hormonal changes in the body, the teen begins to show obvious physical changes like breast development (which most are not very comfortable with),weight gain because of fat retention and muscle build up, body odor, acne, appearance of hair on the face, private part and armpit, and periods for girls etc.

All this shift in appearance can be difficult for some of them to adapt into because this is a new territory for them to tend and explore.

I recall my daughter always feel unhappy when she first starts her period. She will want to stay indoor all through the days of her period for many reasons that does not make sense to me but does to her. Because of the prior understanding I have. I could consistently encourage her and talk her out of that mindset and help her embrace her girly part.

One good thing that can be done as parent is to help them embrace this changes by letting them know that it is normal and every adult has gone through it and other upcoming children will also go through it. It helps a lot to calm their nerves. Help them plan healthy diets and regular exercises also.

## 2. Mood Changes

Increase in hormone level brings about emotional change, they are always emotional about things, they can be very excited or sad, they could be very angry or happy. They are many times overly emotional. Teenagers are often confused because they are not sure whether they are adult or children. Parents see them as children they see themselves as grown up.

At this stage, teenagers become self-conscious, a lot of mood swing , crying is paramount especially in girls, overconfidence or lack of confidence could also surface, their sexual feelings become activated which could make some of them uncomfortable.

As parents listen to them more and give advice only when they ask for it (because they are mostly just looking for an ear to hear) and let them release their frustrations. You will do them a lot of good if you can help arrange good outdoor
activities, this will help them to adjust and adapt very quickly.

## 3. Behavioral Change

Children gain and practice independence during their teenage stage. This may lead them to challenge the rules set forth by the parents and stand up for what they feel is right (this is seen as being argumentative and stubborn).

Teenagers are temperamental, exhausted, and difficult to deal with because their brains are going through significant developmental change. Teenage boys may even be driven to engage in physical tussles by their surging hormones. Furthermore, they would want to boogie out.

Teenagers may desire to explore new things and take risks as a result of their newly found independence, which can lead to reckless behavior.

One of the typical teen behavioral problems is lying. Teenagers may tell lies out of fear or to avoid conflict with their parents. Teenagers behavioral issues can be challenging for parents. But keep in mind that it is just a phase, it will pass, it is perfectly natural.

If you want to assist your teen with behavioral challenges, it's critical to earn their trust. Interact with them and hear what they have to say. Not judging or criticizing them will prevent their behavior from getting worse.

Tell them you love them for who they are. Encourage them to stay true to who they are and they should avoid adopting a personality just to win over others approval. Keep in mind that your teenage child will always need your assistance. Tell them what works for you when you were depressed, angry, or jealous will help them.

They can test those remedies to resolve their own emotional problems.

If you notice them mixing with the wrong kind of people, you'll need to step in and stop it. Keep in mind that teenagers are immature and may not take criticism well.

# BOOK TWO

## HELP THEM OVERCOME THEIR PAINS

My school recently arranged a program for parents of teenagers. Most of the chat was filled with grumblings about parenting teenagers. Each parent was merely adding their grievances to the list and providing no answers.

The majority of articles discuss how to discipline your teen, how to deal with rebellious, defiant, out-of-control, aggressive teens, etc. Very little is written from the perspective of the teenagers.

This made me consider the need for a fresh

perspective on the issue today. This is what I discovered by taking a close look at the teenagers I work with, following them around, speaking to them, and asking them questions.

## Common Problems Affecting Teenagers Everyday

### Body Image Issues

Teenagers are battling to accept their bodies and feel happy in their own bodies as they grow from childhood to adulthood and as their bodies change into different forms and sizes. They are left staring at a stranger in the mirror who is gawky, gangly, hairy, zitty, and unknown after the cherubic infant has vanished. This leads to eating disorder, low self-esteem and negative thoughts about themselves because they are not satisfied with their body image.

## Identity Needs

I see many teenagers struggling to find a place in society, wanting to be recognized by their peers and accepted for what they are. They are dealing with a lot of anxiety and insecurity as they attempt to complete one of the most significant tasks of their lives at this point. The task of who they really are.

Teens may experience feelings of loneliness, alienation, and sadness when they are told that they don't belong and don't fit in. The television programs targeted at this age group normalize aggressive and violent behavior, rule-breaking, premarital sex, bullying, and other negative behaviors.

Only if you engage in some or all of these are you cool. What should a teen do? If they are perplexed, obstinate, or out of control, is it their fault?

## Time-Management Stress

Stress increases at school, and the older they get, the number of projects to be done, tests to cope with, and social drama increases, not to mention sports and other extracurricular activities. On the social front, a new and tantalizing horizon opens up—dating, partying, and hanging out with friends.

Meanwhile, they are constantly distracted by electronic media. A teenager learning to juggle all of these expectations is under a lot of stress. The teen is suddenly expected to act like an adult. They are expected to manage their work independently, make and follow through on the right decisions, and manage their finances.

Though most parents complain about filthy bedrooms, untidy shelves and cabinets, smelly socks, missing stuff, I wonder . . . where is the time!? They simply can't do it all, and the pressure makes them more prone to anxiety and depression.

## Parental and Social Pressure

In many cases, parents want their children to accomplish everything they wanted but didn't have the resources to achieve. It puts a lot of pressure on the teenager to do well in school, have excellent friends, thrive in extracurricular activities, and be responsible for both themselves and possibly for their younger siblings. Also, there is peer pressure. Teenagers experience pressure to conform in their likes, habits, and looks in order to be accepted by classmates and to become "popular." The pressure increases when the teenager feels like everyone around them is trying to change who they are.

Parents, instructors, family members, grandparents, siblings, friends, classmates, and social organizations all have an impact on teenagers and tug them in various directions.

## Depression and Anxiety

A teen is under a lot of emotional stress due to hormonal fluctuations, commotion, and the stress of scheduling, prioritizing, succeeding, and meeting expectations. This manifests as irritability, hostility, depression, anxiety, and occasionally even a total breakdown. There are links between mental and physical wellness. Your teen's psychological well-being will be impacted by his physical health, and vice versa.

## Absence of Decent Role Models

It frequently happens that the worst bullies, wealthiest spoiled brats, and most destructive children are exalted as the most admirable and popular. These individuals are exalted by the media. Depravity is celebrated in media like music, sports, and movies. Everywhere they go, our kids are exposed to bad role models, and they pick up the corrupt morals of the "heroes" they see in the media.

## Alcohol and Drugs

In the US, 33.2% of seniors in high school said they had alcohol recently. In the US, high school adolescents who used marijuana daily were more than 5.9%. According to a specific study on juvenile drug and alcohol usage in the US, nearly 40% of all 12th-graders surveyed had used an illicit drug in the previous year, and 55.7% had consumed alcohol.

Both marijuana and alcohol can harm a teen's developing brain. Talking to them is crucial in order to learn about what is going on at their school and among their friends, learn what they are exposed to, and warn your children about the risks.

## Violence onscreen and harmful social media

Facebook, Instagram, Twitter, and other social media platforms can be fantastic tools for teenagers to connect with the outside world when used responsibly, but when used carelessly, they can cause issues. Video games that are violent encourage hostility and violence. Teens are exposed to violent, sexual, and pornographic content when they use the internet. You can't fully safeguard them no matter what you do. It is still your responsibility as parents to monitor what your children are doing online and teach them safe online behavior.

## Bullying

In the US, 30% of teenagers have experienced bullying, either as a victim or a perpetrator. In the US, 1 in 3 teenagers report experiencing bullying at school, but bullying is also prevalent online. Most people are unaware that bullying can be direct or indirect, which involves spreading rumors and engaging in gossip. Many children aren't even aware of what cyberbullying is, let alone completely comprehend the potentially negative consequences of their online actions.

## Risky sexual behavior and activity

More than 50 percent of US youths have had sex by the time they turn 18 years old, as reported by the National Center for Health Statistics (NCHS). Despite the recent drop in teen pregnancies, this does not always indicate that they are utilizing contraception. More than half of the 20 million new STD diagnoses each year affect those between the ages of 15 and 24. Surveys regularly reveal that most parents do not believe their children are sexually active, despite the evidence. Again, even if you don't believe your children are having sex, it's crucial to talk to them about it.

# BOOK THREE

## Parenting Made Easy

Teenagers love their privacy and does not like to share their life with just anyone only those they trust. They many times believe that what they are going through is only unique to them and no other person has gone through it. They are on the quest of finding themselves and they always desire to find someone to trust, someone they can relate with (someone they can flow together, someone that understand them.)

Most of them do not see parents fit into this role or picture. 80% will open up to somebody else than their parents and this hurts our feelings many times as parent.

It's a common trend now to have disagreement, misunderstanding between teens and their parents. We will discuss several tips that can help us have the trust of our children and make them our friends for life.

## 1. Try not to be bossy

Teens don't like to be controlled (actually nobody does). Does this mean you will leave them to roam? NO. Don't make it look like you want to help them live their lives. Let them see and understand that you only want to guide them through the path because you have gone through it before therefore you have experience to help them learn and keep safe.

As parent learn not to LORD things over them but help them see why. As time goes by they will trust you and your judgment enough

## 2. Build a trust relationship

This is a relationship that require time and cannot be rushed. Does your teen trust you? If no build a trust relationship with them and develop it. How? When you promise keep to it. Don't lie in their presence and when you say a thing make sure you stand by it. This will help them to trust you.

If you are a parent and your children are not yet teen please work on your trust relationship, be your children best friend. It helps a lot to get along with them in days to come.

## 3. Be their role model and pals

One of the hunger in a teanager's heart is who to model and pattern their life after. Be their hero,especially treat your parents the way you want your children to treat you,they will copy your lifestyle by watching you.

Make being your children’s best friend one of your parenting goals. Start early with them and it is never too late to start if that has not been achieved in your home. Statistic shows that many teen believe that their parents don’t understand them.  Which always lead to friction and argument. If you bound with them early in life in friendship, it curbs and win over misunderstanding and disagreement that is associated with this stage, also this relationship will last through out ones life. Life pattern picked from early years hardly change.

## 4. Handle them with patients

Teen are full of emotional hormones, they display all manners of attitude. They see themselves more right and they see you parents as always wrong. Their thought life is coming superly alive and active, so they have a lot going on inside them. Deal with them patiently but firmly

## 5. Be firm but gentle

Let there be rules which when broken has penalty. But kindly let them know their wrongs, tell it to them in a gentle tone and not harshly, not in anger and make them go through appropriate discipline. I want to give it to you that tones especially  gentle and kind tone does a lot of magic on teens, it readily calm them than force or angry tone.parents will only be a able to model their children's life through gentleness.

## 6. Be an example

Teenagers are always on the constant search for a role model, a hero and someone to look up to. They follow many times unconsciously and there are times they follow deliberately. Make every effort to be their first role model, be that which you want them to be. You want them to be respectful treat people with respect.

Learn not to argue or exchange words as a couple in the presence of your children, this will help them to respect you parents and others around them.

Apple does not fall far from its tree. Many times children give back to us what they have learnt from us.

If you want your teen to be kind practice kindness both in their presence and absence. Be what you want your children to be.

## 7. Be up to date

Don't be too occupied with work that you are not updated with current news, development and technologies around you.

You may not know in details but always know some of the latest development around you.

It helps your conversions to flow more and when there is conversation you will know them more and better

## 8. Don't always conclude too soon

I don't I like to be judged or not given element of doubt, I don't about you. Most teens are also like this, they love to be given opportunity to explain themselves. When you hear anything about them or you observe anything, give them room to explain themselves and don't make it so obvious even when you don't believe what they say.

## 9. Spend time together

Children will form bond with whom they spend much time. Begin from early years so that the pattern can continue to adulthood and in the lineage. Learn to shed some engagement to spend time together, it does not have to be a vacation, if you have not been spending quality and meaningful time together before, vacation will be boring and be a waste of time.

## 10. No Comparison

Everyone love to standout and be uniquely different including me. The beauty of life is that we are all uniquely different. Identical twins are not identical in character. Please deliberately learn the attitude of not comparing your teen with any other person be it their immediate siblings or friends, it piss them off readily. The early you realize the uniqueness of individuals the ease with your coping with your children's different behaviors.

## 11. Be Confident

Don't allow fear to rule your life and control you. When fear is involved you will want your teen to not live your failure. Accept your past, live your present and embrace the future.

## 12. Allow them to experience failure

This is always a challenge. It is never fun to

see someone you care about lose, get harmed, or fail but failure is crucial for your teen's growth and development. Failure teaches us all more than victory does.

## 13. Don't tolerate disrespect

The boundaries between teenagers and parents and other authority figures are blurred in our culture because of how casual everything is. Words like "Just joking" and "I didn't mean it" should not be allowed to cover rudeness. It can be difficult to figure out how to make our children appreciate us because we don't want to drive them away by micromanaging every action.

But this does not mean we should tolerate rudeness and disrespect. Draw the line and let them do the needful when they cross the line.

## 14. Learn to let go

Don’t take it much to heart when your teenagers prefer to hang out with others rather than you, it could be difficult to come in terms with it but learn to release them as long as it is a healthy relationship. When they need to leave the house let them don’t keep them back because of fear and insecurity, this may be difficult but allow it and you will be glad you did.

## 15. Study your teenager to know them

Take time to study your children especially

at this teenage stage. This will help you to know their strength, weakness, struggles, what can readily disrupt their emotions and personality. When you do this it make staying connected easy and resolving any conflict or disagreement very fast

## 16. Answer all their questions

As our children grows their understanding also do, therefore all sought of questions will be popping up especially at teenage level a lot of questions is in their heart. i will like to advice that, you should not avoid any conversation with them no matter how tough it may appear. They need to hear the constructive and well-structured answer to their questions. If you avoid it they will still get answers but mostly at a price.

## 17. Let your teen go through the consequences of their actions

We make mistakes once in a while. But when we make the same mistake repeatedly, it becomes a habit. You need to help your teenagers learn from their mistakes, how? By letting them go through the natural consequences of their actions, as far as possible. Your teenager will be less motivated to get out of bed on time if she is aware that you will drive her to school any time she misses the bus.

The same is true if you ask a teacher to permit your teenager to retake an exam in the name that he receives a poor grade.

If you keep doing this, he won't establish the study habits required to succeed in school. Every parent wants to protect their children from suffering. But occasionally the most effective technique to impart a lesson in life is to let children go through the repercussions of their decisions or actions

## 18. Do not engage them in conversation when angry

Imagine the following scene:

Your teen sneaked out of the house at night, without any message or note. The mobile phone is switched off and no how to contact him/her. Your anxiety will turns into rage when you uncovered what actually happen. In this scenario, most parents would grand their teen or sit their teens down and immediately start lecturing them about their irresponsible behavior. Truly the child/teen is wrong but once you lash out in anger the teen's auto defensive mind will be activated and their reception mind will also shut down. Engaging in any positive or meaningful conversation will be very impossible at this time.

Try to have these difficult conversations when both you and your teen are calm. Your teens need to understand what mistakes they made, this very important, But it's always easier to teach a lesson when your own emotions aren’t getting in the way.

## 19. Aid your teen in pursuing their passions and interests.

Do you not grasp your teen's hobby and interest? Do you constantly remind your teen to focus and be "productive"? This should not always be. As long as your teenagers have adequate time management skills, try your best to encourage their interests. To begin, pay attention to their interests and pastimes. Allow them to pick the Friday night movie or you can play their favorite music with them.

By doing this, you can demonstrate to your teenagers that you actually want to know them better, which is a valuable gift.

## 20. Eat meals together frequently

It is cannot be refute or disputed that spending time regularly as a family over meals have many advantages. Especially immediate family.

- According to research, eating meals together as a family:
- Decreases incidence of substance misuse/abuse, anxiety, depression and sadness. Promotes physical wellness, fortitude and self-worth.

- Decreases the likelihood of substance misuse, teenage pregnancy, and smoking

Furthermore, 80% of teenagers claim that they are most likely to talk to their parents during family mealtimes. Mealtimes are a great time to talk to your teenagers if you want to improve communication. You shouldn't ignore this easy parenting advice for teens.

## 21. Concentrate on what is essential

Do you dislike the haircut your teenager has? Does she favor outfits that leave you rolling your eyes? Even the most responsible teenagers are learning about their individuality and personalities, so resist the need to attempt to manage your teenager's life. So, when it comes to raising teenagers, conserve your strength for the long-term priorities.

## 22. Recognize your teen's positive tendencies and habits

You might be thinking that your teen doesn't exhibit any positive behaviors or habits, and I understand! It's simple to criticize your teenagers, especially when you're trying to teach them positive behaviors that will help them succeed in life. Nevertheless, it's beneficial to stand back and appreciate all the amazing things your teenagers do, no matter how minor they may be.

Recognize it if you see your teenagers studying diligently or tidying their beds in the morning. Teen motivation can be increased with descriptive praise.Even though your teenagers don't seem to care what you think, know that they do. Teenagers long for the trustworthy adults' approval, but if they believe they will never receive it, they may give up.

## 23. Keep in touch with your teenager, but be mindful of his or her privacy

Keep in touch with your teenager, but be mindful of his or her privacy. It's important to be aware of what is happening in your adolescents' lives. You'll want to know if they're engaging in harmful behavior or spending time with undesirable people so you can help them make better choices.

The greatest method to stay informed about your teen's life isn't to read her diary or intrude on her privacy. Instead, remain involved and present with your teenagers. Interact with them. Engage them in activities they like to do. When they grumble or express their annoyance, pay attention to them. Teenagers are more inclined to come to you with issues if you demonstrate that you respect their autonomy and privacy.

## 24. Promote self-care

Teenagers must strive to learn well and obtain good scores, but they must also maintain a healthy balance in their personal and academic lives.

Inform your teenagers on the benefits of sleep, good eating, and exercise. You'll have a hard time getting your teenagers to do anything constructive if they don't feel good physically. The right kind of self-care will also help them focus and use their time more effectively. Encourage your teenagers to develop healthy coping mechanisms for stress and anxiety. They will then develop into healthy individuals who know how to look after themselves and act in ways that are also beneficial to others.

## 25. Never hesitate to show vulnerability

Remember to demonstrate to your teenagers that you are also a human being. There isn't a perfect parent out there! Making errors as a teen parent is OK. Show vulnerability rather than acting like you have it all figured out. When you make a mistake, beg for forgiveness. Show your teen that learning and growth are more important than being flawless in life.

***NOTICE:*** *THIS IS STRICTLY FOR THOSE WHO BELIEVES IN PRAYER OR CHRISTAINS*

Pray daily for your teen, commit their heart to God and remove every wrong seeds, influence or ideals that contradict the life of Christ through constant prayers. This works a lot for most of the teens I have worked with.

# BOOK FOUR

## Save Them From Themselves

We have already discussed some of the common changes teen goes through and how you can systematically win them back. Teenagers must be disciplined if their developing attitudes are to be regulated. Your teenager could develop poor habits and succumb to peer pressure if you don't exercise discipline.

# How to Effectively Discipline Your Teens

## Firmly But Reasonably Ground Them

Grounding kids is a tried-and-true method of discipline. It could be your last resort. If they continue to party into the early hours of the morning despite repeated warnings you can ground them but do not ground them for trivial reasons.

## Withdraw Privileges

It's time to show your teenager the value of the comforts they enjoy if they take your love and attention for granted. However, make sure you explain your reasons to them before you suspend their privileges.

Otherwise, your teen can make erroneous assumptions and raise a fuss. Additionally, don't go too far; set a time boundary.

## Your Rules, Your Territory

It's appropriate for your teenager to periodically make decisions and manage their own lives. But anything in excess can be detrimental. It's time to be assertive with your teenager if they repeatedly defy your rules and make fun of you for telling them what's right and wrong. Tell them that everything will happen according to your rules because it is your home.

## Let Them Deal With The Repercussions

The finest teacher is experience. It's sometimes advisable to let your teenager deal with the results of their behavior. But make sure that your child takes something positive out of the experience. In order to prevent your teen from getting into trouble again, talk to them and get their perception over the situation.

## Do Not Give Orders

Teenagers frequently rebel and object when you give them orders. For instance, if you ask your teenager, "Tell me where you are going," they can stamp their feet and walk away.

The best way to reprimand them is to say, "I worry about you; it would help me settle down if you told me where you are going."

## Let Them Fix The Problems

Giving your teenager the opportunity to make apologies is a further means of correcting their behavior. Make a plan to allow them to make up for any harm or damage they have caused. It could involve making apologies to the person they have injured or putting in extra time to compensate for the harm. They will be forced to consider the consequences of their behavior, and they might hesitate before making such a mistake again.

## Increase Their Responsibilities

Do you want your adolescent to recognize the worth of something? Increase their responsibilities. Make your teenager cook dinner for the entire family, for instance, if they snort and frown when you prepare a decent meal after working two shifts.

## Be Their Friend

This may not seem like a method of punishment, but it accomplishes more than just correcting your kid. Gaining your teen's trust will be much easier if you become friends with them. Spend time with them to demonstrate your regard for and comprehension of their emotions.

The quickest way to make friends with your

teenager is to participate in something you both enjoy. Do not lose heart if your teen prefers to spend more time with their friends and keep some aspects of their life hidden from you; this is entirely normal. You might experience ache, but give them time to figure it out.

**In conclusion;**

Although raising teenagers is challenging, I have no doubt that you'll succeed if you use the advice in this literature. Continue giving it your all, and you'll prepare your children for success and happiness throughout their entire life.

ACKNOWLEDGEMENT

I want to thank God for the help He gave to complete this work, Lord I am grateful.

I also want to appreciate my husband and friend for me to be a dependable mother and best friends of our two children, Shalom and Salem.

I appreciate my parents for their sacrifices to bring me up correctly and honorably, I am forever indebted to you,  your unending love and patience, you are the best.

For all the children and students that have passed through my hands and allowed me to build this wealth of experience I say thank you and I love you all.

# ABOUT THE AUTHOR

Deborah Grace is happily married with children and a high school teacher. She has been working with teenagers as a tutor and coach for more than 10 years.

She specializes in Science, Chemistry and Educational Psychology.

Debby is very passionate about helping teenagers grow up into responsible and respectable young adults and helping parents understand and connect with their teens better.

For twelve years she has been able to: Help teens rediscover their lives purpose, Guide them on how to overcome negative influence. Help them build their resilience and self-esteem.

Her students have always appreciated her style of treating them with respect and love, her desire to help more parents understand and connect more effectively with their teenagers birth this book.

www.ingramcontent.com/pod-product-compliance
Lightning Source LLC
LaVergne TN
LVHW052059160826
845678LV00015B/3294

* 9 7 9 8 3 5 2 4 9 7 3 4 0 *